PODCAST PLANNER

THE LITTLE GUIDED PLANNER TO A
SUCCESSFUL PODCAST

JERRY "THE POD-STARTER"
HAMILTON

© Copyright 2020 - All rights reserved Admore Publishing

ISBN: 978-3-96772-014-3

The content contained within this book may not be reproduced, duplicated or transmitted without direct written permission from the author or the publisher.

Under no circumstances will any blame or legal responsibility be held against the publisher, or author, for any damages, reparation, or monetary loss due to the information contained within this book. Either directly or indirectly.

Cover artwork by "Freepik" from www.flaticon.com

Published by Admore Publishing: Roßbachstraße, Berlin, Germany

Printed in the United States of America

www.publishing.admore-marketing.com

CONTENTS

Foreword   v

1. Audience & Niche Selection   1
2. Branding   9
3. Goals   13
4. Monthly Planner   17
5. Episode Planner   31

Also By Jerry   139

FOREWORD

Hi, my name is Jerry and I absolutely love helping people get their message out there!

At its core, podcasting is a format that allows just that. To get your message out there in its purest form. Unfiltered, serious, dramatic, funny, informative... raw. There are no limits with podcasts.

I believe everyone has a unique story to tell that brings value to the world. This planner will help you start your podcasting journey and plan out your first 100 episodes.

You can use this planner by itself, but it also works great in combination with my podcast guide: "The Little Book of Podcasting".

Foreword

This book is dedicated entirely to teaching you all I know about starting a podcast. It is organized in 7 simple steps that walk you from selecting a niche to finally hitting publish. Read on for straight to the point guidance along with plenty of tips and tricks.

Now let's get started with planning your podcast.

AUDIENCE & NICHE Selection

BRAINSTORM
Session

WHAT ARE 5-20 NICHES YOU COULD
START A PODCAST IN?

Notes:

BRAINSTORM
Session

WHAT ARE PROBLEMS WITHIN EACH
NICHE... IDEAS... TALKING POINTS?

Notes:

BRAINSTORM
Session

DEFINE YOUR AUDIENCE

Notes:

BRANDING

Your Podcast Brand!

Values

Style (Colors, Voice, etc.)

Community

Extra Notes

Notes:

GOALS

Podcast Goals!

1 Month

6 Month

1 Year

3 Years

Notes:

MONTHLY
Planner

MONTHLY *Planner*

Month _____

SUN	MON	TUE	WED	THU	FRI	SAT

Monthly Goals:

MONTHLY *Planner*

Month _____

SUN	MON	TUE	WED	THU	FRI	SAT

Monthly Goals:

MONTHLY *Planner*

Month _____

SUN	MON	TUE	WED	THU	FRI	SAT

Monthly Goals:

MONTHLY *Planner*

Month _____

SUN	MON	TUE	WED	THU	FRI	SAT

Monthly Goals:

MONTHLY *Planner*

Month _____

SUN	MON	TUE	WED	THU	FRI	SAT

Monthly Goals:

MONTHLY *Planner*

Month _____

SUN	MON	TUE	WED	THU	FRI	SAT

Monthly Goals:

MONTHLY *Planner*

Month _____

SUN	MON	TUE	WED	THU	FRI	SAT

Monthly Goals:

MONTHLY *Planner*

Month _____

SUN	MON	TUE	WED	THU	FRI	SAT

Monthly Goals:

MONTHLY *Planner*

Month _____

SUN	MON	TUE	WED	THU	FRI	SAT

Monthly Goals:

MONTHLY *Planner*

Month _____

SUN	MON	TUE	WED	THU	FRI	SAT

Monthly Goals:

MONTHLY *Planner*

Month _____

SUN	MON	TUE	WED	THU	FRI	SAT

Monthly Goals:

MONTHLY *Planner*

Month _____

SUN	MON	TUE	WED	THU	FRI	SAT

Monthly Goals:

EPISODE
Planner

EPISODE *Planner*

TITLE

DISCRIPTION

GUEST **DATE**

SCRIPT/NOTES

KEYWORDS

CHECKLIST:
- ☐ Record ☐ Live on Directories
- ☐ Edit ☐ Marketing
- ☐ Publish on Host ☐ Monetized

EPISODE *Planner*

TITLE

DISCRIPTION

GUEST   DATE

SCRIPT/NOTES

KEYWORDS   CHECKLIST:
- [ ] Record   - [ ] Live on Directories
- [ ] Edit   - [ ] Marketing
- [ ] Publish on Host - [ ] Monetized

EPISODE *Planner*

TITLE

DISCRIPTION

GUEST   DATE

SCRIPT/NOTES

KEYWORDS   CHECKLIST:
                     ☐ Record   ☐ Live on Directories
                     ☐ Edit   ☐ Marketing
                     ☐ Publish on Host   ☐ Monetized

EPISODE *Planner*

TITLE

DISCRIPTION

GUEST   DATE

SCRIPT/NOTES

KEYWORDS   CHECKLIST:
- [ ] Record   [ ] Live on Directories
- [ ] Edit   [ ] Marketing
- [ ] Publish on Host [ ] Monetized

EPISODE *Planner*

TITLE

DISCRIPTION

GUEST   DATE

SCRIPT/NOTES

KEYWORDS   CHECKLIST:
- [ ] Record   - [ ] Live on Directories
- [ ] Edit   - [ ] Marketing
- [ ] Publish on Host - [ ] Monetized

EPISODE *Planner*

TITLE

DISCRIPTION

GUEST   DATE

SCRIPT/NOTES

KEYWORDS

CHECKLIST:
- [ ] Record
- [ ] Live on Directories
- [ ] Edit
- [ ] Marketing
- [ ] Publish on Host
- [ ] Monetized

EPISODE *Planner*

TITLE

DISCRIPTION

GUEST   DATE

SCRIPT/NOTES

KEYWORDS   CHECKLIST:
- ☐ Record   ☐ Live on Directories
- ☐ Edit   ☐ Marketing
- ☐ Publish on Host   ☐ Monetized

EPISODE *Planner*

TITLE

DISCRIPTION

GUEST   **DATE**

SCRIPT/NOTES

KEYWORDS

CHECKLIST:
- ☐ Record   ☐ Live on Directories
- ☐ Edit   ☐ Marketing
- ☐ Publish on Host ☐ Monetized

EPISODE *Planner*

TITLE

DISCRIPTION

GUEST   DATE

SCRIPT/NOTES

KEYWORDS   CHECKLIST:
- ☐ Record   ☐ Live on Directories
- ☐ Edit   ☐ Marketing
- ☐ Publish on Host ☐ Monetized

EPISODE *Planner*

TITLE

DISCRIPTION

GUEST   DATE

SCRIPT/NOTES

KEYWORDS   CHECKLIST:
- ☐ Record   ☐ Live on Directories
- ☐ Edit   ☐ Marketing
- ☐ Publish on Host   ☐ Monetized

EPISODE *Planner*

TITLE

DISCRIPTION

GUEST **DATE**

SCRIPT/NOTES

KEYWORDS

CHECKLIST:
- ☐ Record ☐ Live on Directories
- ☐ Edit ☐ Marketing
- ☐ Publish on Host ☐ Monetized

EPISODE *Planner*

TITLE

DISCRIPTION

GUEST   DATE

SCRIPT/NOTES

KEYWORDS

CHECKLIST:
- [ ] Record
- [ ] Edit
- [ ] Publish on Host
- [ ] Live on Directories
- [ ] Marketing
- [ ] Monetized

EPISODE *Planner*

TITLE

DISCRIPTION

GUEST   DATE

SCRIPT/NOTES

KEYWORDS   CHECKLIST:
- ☐ Record   ☐ Live on Directories
- ☐ Edit   ☐ Marketing
- ☐ Publish on Host   ☐ Monetized

EPISODE *Planner*

TITLE

DISCRIPTION

GUEST   DATE

SCRIPT/NOTES

KEYWORDS   CHECKLIST:
- [ ] Record   　　[ ] Live on Directories
- [ ] Edit   　　　[ ] Marketing
- [ ] Publish on Host [ ] Monetized

EPISODE *Planner*

TITLE

DISCRIPTION

GUEST   DATE

SCRIPT/NOTES

KEYWORDS   CHECKLIST:
- ☐ Record   ☐ Live on Directories
- ☐ Edit   ☐ Marketing
- ☐ Publish on Host ☐ Monetized

EPISODE *Planner*

TITLE

DISCRIPTION

GUEST   **DATE**

SCRIPT/NOTES

KEYWORDS

CHECKLIST:
- ☐ Record
- ☐ Edit
- ☐ Publish on Host
- ☐ Live on Directories
- ☐ Marketing
- ☐ Monetized

EPISODE *Planner*

TITLE

DISCRIPTION

GUEST   DATE

SCRIPT/NOTES

KEYWORDS   CHECKLIST:
- ☐ Record   ☐ Live on Directories
- ☐ Edit   ☐ Marketing
- ☐ Publish on Host ☐ Monetized

EPISODE *Planner*

TITLE

DISCRIPTION

GUEST   DATE

SCRIPT/NOTES

KEYWORDS   CHECKLIST:
- ☐ Record   ☐ Live on Directories
- ☐ Edit   ☐ Marketing
- ☐ Publish on Host ☐ Monetized

EPISODE *Planner*

TITLE

DISCRIPTION

GUEST   DATE

SCRIPT/NOTES

KEYWORDS   CHECKLIST:
- [ ] Record   [ ] Live on Directories
- [ ] Edit   [ ] Marketing
- [ ] Publish on Host [ ] Monetized

EPISODE *Planner*

TITLE

DISCRIPTION

GUEST   **DATE**

SCRIPT/NOTES

KEYWORDS   **CHECKLIST:**

- ☐ Record   ☐ Live on Directories
- ☐ Edit   ☐ Marketing
- ☐ Publish on Host   ☐ Monetized

EPISODE *Planner*

TITLE

DISCRIPTION

GUEST   DATE

SCRIPT/NOTES

KEYWORDS   CHECKLIST:
- ☐ Record   ☐ Live on Directories
- ☐ Edit   ☐ Marketing
- ☐ Publish on Host ☐ Monetized

EPISODE *Planner*

TITLE

DISCRIPTION

GUEST   DATE

SCRIPT/NOTES

KEYWORDS   CHECKLIST:
- ☐ Record   ☐ Live on Directories
- ☐ Edit   ☐ Marketing
- ☐ Publish on Host ☐ Monetized

EPISODE *Planner*

TITLE

DISCRIPTION

GUEST   **DATE**

SCRIPT/NOTES

KEYWORDS   **CHECKLIST:**
- ☐ Record   ☐ Live on Directories
- ☐ Edit   ☐ Marketing
- ☐ Publish on Host   ☐ Monetized

EPISODE *Planner*

TITLE

DISCRIPTION

GUEST   DATE

SCRIPT/NOTES

KEYWORDS   CHECKLIST:
- ☐ Record   ☐ Live on Directories
- ☐ Edit   ☐ Marketing
- ☐ Publish on Host ☐ Monetized

EPISODE *Planner*

TITLE

DISCRIPTION

GUEST   DATE

SCRIPT/NOTES

KEYWORDS   CHECKLIST:
                  ☐ Record   ☐ Live on Directories
                  ☐ Edit   ☐ Marketing
                  ☐ Publish on Host   ☐ Monetized

EPISODE *Planner*

TITLE

DISCRIPTION

GUEST **DATE**

SCRIPT/NOTES

KEYWORDS

CHECKLIST:
- ☐ Record
- ☐ Edit
- ☐ Publish on Host
- ☐ Live on Directories
- ☐ Marketing
- ☐ Monetized

EPISODE *Planner*

TITLE

DISCRIPTION

GUEST   DATE

SCRIPT/NOTES

KEYWORDS   CHECKLIST:
- ☐ Record   ☐ Live on Directories
- ☐ Edit   ☐ Marketing
- ☐ Publish on Host ☐ Monetized

EPISODE *Planner*

TITLE

DISCRIPTION

GUEST   DATE

SCRIPT/NOTES

KEYWORDS   CHECKLIST:
- ☐ Record   ☐ Live on Directories
- ☐ Edit   ☐ Marketing
- ☐ Publish on Host   ☐ Monetized

EPISODE *Planner*

TITLE

DISCRIPTION

GUEST   DATE

SCRIPT/NOTES

KEYWORDS

CHECKLIST:
- ☐ Record
- ☐ Edit
- ☐ Publish on Host
- ☐ Live on Directories
- ☐ Marketing
- ☐ Monetized

EPISODE *Planner*

TITLE

DISCRIPTION

GUEST **DATE**

SCRIPT/NOTES

KEYWORDS

CHECKLIST:
- ☐ Record
- ☐ Edit
- ☐ Publish on Host
- ☐ Live on Directories
- ☐ Marketing
- ☐ Monetized

EPISODE *Planner*

TITLE

DISCRIPTION

GUEST   **DATE**

SCRIPT/NOTES

KEYWORDS   **CHECKLIST:**

- ☐ Record   ☐ Live on Directories
- ☐ Edit   ☐ Marketing
- ☐ Publish on Host   ☐ Monetized

EPISODE *Planner*

TITLE

DISCRIPTION

GUEST   DATE

SCRIPT/NOTES

KEYWORDS   CHECKLIST:
                 ☐ Record   ☐ Live on Directories
                 ☐ Edit   ☐ Marketing
                 ☐ Publish on Host   ☐ Monetized

EPISODE *Planner*

TITLE

DISCRIPTION

GUEST   DATE

SCRIPT/NOTES

KEYWORDS   CHECKLIST:
- ☐ Record   ☐ Live on Directories
- ☐ Edit   ☐ Marketing
- ☐ Publish on Host ☐ Monetized

EPISODE *Planner*

TITLE

DISCRIPTION

GUEST **DATE**

SCRIPT/NOTES

KEYWORDS

CHECKLIST:
- ☐ Record
- ☐ Edit
- ☐ Publish on Host
- ☐ Live on Directories
- ☐ Marketing
- ☐ Monetized

EPISODE *Planner*

TITLE

DISCRIPTION

GUEST **DATE**

SCRIPT/NOTES

KEYWORDS

CHECKLIST:
- ☐ Record
- ☐ Edit
- ☐ Publish on Host
- ☐ Live on Directories
- ☐ Marketing
- ☐ Monetized

EPISODE *Planner*

TITLE

DISCRIPTION

GUEST   DATE

SCRIPT/NOTES

KEYWORDS   CHECKLIST:
- [ ] Record   [ ] Live on Directories
- [ ] Edit   [ ] Marketing
- [ ] Publish on Host [ ] Monetized

EPISODE *Planner*

TITLE

DISCRIPTION

GUEST   **DATE**

SCRIPT/NOTES

KEYWORDS   **CHECKLIST:**
- ☐ Record   ☐ Live on Directories
- ☐ Edit   ☐ Marketing
- ☐ Publish on Host   ☐ Monetized

EPISODE *Planner*

TITLE

DISCRIPTION

GUEST   **DATE**

SCRIPT/NOTES

KEYWORDS

CHECKLIST:
- ☐ Record   ☐ Live on Directories
- ☐ Edit   ☐ Marketing
- ☐ Publish on Host ☐ Monetized

EPISODE *Planner*

TITLE

DISCRIPTION

GUEST   DATE

SCRIPT/NOTES

KEYWORDS

CHECKLIST:
- [ ] Record
- [ ] Edit
- [ ] Publish on Host
- [ ] Live on Directories
- [ ] Marketing
- [ ] Monetized

EPISODE *Planner*

TITLE

DISCRIPTION

GUEST   DATE

SCRIPT/NOTES

KEYWORDS

CHECKLIST:
- ☐ Record   ☐ Live on Directories
- ☐ Edit   ☐ Marketing
- ☐ Publish on Host ☐ Monetized

EPISODE *Planner*

TITLE

DISCRIPTION

GUEST **DATE**

SCRIPT/NOTES

KEYWORDS

CHECKLIST:
- ☐ Record
- ☐ Edit
- ☐ Publish on Host
- ☐ Live on Directories
- ☐ Marketing
- ☐ Monetized

EPISODE *Planner*

TITLE

DISCRIPTION

GUEST   DATE

SCRIPT/NOTES

KEYWORDS   CHECKLIST:
- [ ] Record   - [ ] Live on Directories
- [ ] Edit   - [ ] Marketing
- [ ] Publish on Host - [ ] Monetized

EPISODE *Planner*

TITLE

DISCRIPTION

GUEST   DATE

SCRIPT/NOTES

KEYWORDS

CHECKLIST:
- [ ] Record   - [ ] Live on Directories
- [ ] Edit   - [ ] Marketing
- [ ] Publish on Host - [ ] Monetized

EPISODE *Planner*

TITLE

DISCRIPTION

GUEST   DATE

SCRIPT/NOTES

KEYWORDS   CHECKLIST:
- ☐ Record   ☐ Live on Directories
- ☐ Edit   ☐ Marketing
- ☐ Publish on Host   ☐ Monetized

EPISODE *Planner*

TITLE

DISCRIPTION

GUEST   DATE

SCRIPT/NOTES

KEYWORDS   CHECKLIST:
- ☐ Record   ☐ Live on Directories
- ☐ Edit   ☐ Marketing
- ☐ Publish on Host   ☐ Monetized

EPISODE *Planner*

TITLE

DISCRIPTION

GUEST   **DATE**

SCRIPT/NOTES

KEYWORDS   **CHECKLIST:**
- ☐ Record   ☐ Live on Directories
- ☐ Edit   ☐ Marketing
- ☐ Publish on Host   ☐ Monetized

EPISODE *Planner*

TITLE

DISCRIPTION

GUEST   DATE

SCRIPT/NOTES

KEYWORDS   CHECKLIST:
- ☐ Record   ☐ Live on Directories
- ☐ Edit   ☐ Marketing
- ☐ Publish on Host ☐ Monetized

EPISODE *Planner*

TITLE

DISCRIPTION

GUEST **DATE**

SCRIPT/NOTES

KEYWORDS

CHECKLIST:
- ☐ Record
- ☐ Edit
- ☐ Publish on Host
- ☐ Live on Directories
- ☐ Marketing
- ☐ Monetized

EPISODE *Planner*

TITLE

DISCRIPTION

GUEST **DATE**

SCRIPT/NOTES

KEYWORDS

CHECKLIST:
- ☐ Record ☐ Live on Directories
- ☐ Edit ☐ Marketing
- ☐ Publish on Host ☐ Monetized

EPISODE *Planner*

TITLE

DISCRIPTION

GUEST **DATE**

SCRIPT/NOTES

KEYWORDS

CHECKLIST:
- ☐ Record ☐ Live on Directories
- ☐ Edit ☐ Marketing
- ☐ Publish on Host ☐ Monetized

EPISODE *Planner*

TITLE

DISCRIPTION

GUEST   DATE

SCRIPT/NOTES

KEYWORDS   CHECKLIST:
- [ ] Record   [ ] Live on Directories
- [ ] Edit   [ ] Marketing
- [ ] Publish on Host [ ] Monetized

EPISODE *Planner*

TITLE

DISCRIPTION

GUEST   DATE

SCRIPT/NOTES

KEYWORDS   CHECKLIST:
- ☐ Record   ☐ Live on Directories
- ☐ Edit   ☐ Marketing
- ☐ Publish on Host   ☐ Monetized

EPISODE *Planner*

TITLE

DISCRIPTION

GUEST   DATE

SCRIPT/NOTES

KEYWORDS   CHECKLIST:
- ☐ Record   ☐ Live on Directories
- ☐ Edit   ☐ Marketing
- ☐ Publish on Host   ☐ Monetized

EPISODE *Planner*

TITLE

DISCRIPTION

GUEST   DATE

SCRIPT/NOTES

KEYWORDS   CHECKLIST:
- ☐ Record   ☐ Live on Directories
- ☐ Edit   ☐ Marketing
- ☐ Publish on Host ☐ Monetized

EPISODE *Planner*

TITLE

DISCRIPTION

GUEST　　　　　　　　　　　　　　**DATE**

SCRIPT/NOTES

KEYWORDS

CHECKLIST:
- ☐ Record
- ☐ Edit
- ☐ Publish on Host
- ☐ Live on Directories
- ☐ Marketing
- ☐ Monetized

EPISODE *Planner*

TITLE

DISCRIPTION

GUEST **DATE**

SCRIPT/NOTES

KEYWORDS

CHECKLIST:
- ☐ Record
- ☐ Edit
- ☐ Publish on Host
- ☐ Live on Directories
- ☐ Marketing
- ☐ Monetized

EPISODE *Planner*

TITLE

DISCRIPTION

GUEST   DATE

SCRIPT/NOTES

KEYWORDS   CHECKLIST:
- ☐ Record   ☐ Live on Directories
- ☐ Edit   ☐ Marketing
- ☐ Publish on Host   ☐ Monetized

EPISODE *Planner*

TITLE

DISCRIPTION

GUEST   **DATE**

SCRIPT/NOTES

KEYWORDS   **CHECKLIST:**
- ☐ Record   ☐ Live on Directories
- ☐ Edit   ☐ Marketing
- ☐ Publish on Host   ☐ Monetized

EPISODE *Planner*

TITLE

DISCRIPTION

GUEST   DATE

SCRIPT/NOTES

KEYWORDS   CHECKLIST:
- ☐ Record   ☐ Live on Directories
- ☐ Edit   ☐ Marketing
- ☐ Publish on Host   ☐ Monetized

EPISODE *Planner*

TITLE

DISCRIPTION

GUEST   DATE

SCRIPT/NOTES

KEYWORDS   CHECKLIST:
                  ☐ Record   ☐ Live on Directories
                  ☐ Edit   ☐ Marketing
                  ☐ Publish on Host   ☐ Monetized

EPISODE *Planner*

TITLE

DISCRIPTION

GUEST **DATE**

SCRIPT/NOTES

KEYWORDS

CHECKLIST:
- ☐ Record
- ☐ Edit
- ☐ Publish on Host
- ☐ Live on Directories
- ☐ Marketing
- ☐ Monetized

EPISODE *Planner*

TITLE

DISCRIPTION

GUEST **DATE**

SCRIPT/NOTES

KEYWORDS

CHECKLIST:
- ☐ Record   ☐ Live on Directories
- ☐ Edit   ☐ Marketing
- ☐ Publish on Host ☐ Monetized

EPISODE *Planner*

TITLE

DISCRIPTION

GUEST   DATE

SCRIPT/NOTES

KEYWORDS   CHECKLIST:
- ☐ Record   ☐ Live on Directories
- ☐ Edit   ☐ Marketing
- ☐ Publish on Host ☐ Monetized

EPISODE *Planner*

TITLE

DISCRIPTION

GUEST   **DATE**

SCRIPT/NOTES

KEYWORDS   **CHECKLIST:**
- ☐ Record   ☐ Live on Directories
- ☐ Edit   ☐ Marketing
- ☐ Publish on Host ☐ Monetized

EPISODE *Planner*

TITLE

DISCRIPTION

GUEST   **DATE**

SCRIPT/NOTES

KEYWORDS   **CHECKLIST:**
- [ ] Record   - [ ] Live on Directories
- [ ] Edit   - [ ] Marketing
- [ ] Publish on Host   - [ ] Monetized

EPISODE *Planner*

TITLE

DISCRIPTION

GUEST **DATE**

SCRIPT/NOTES

KEYWORDS

CHECKLIST:
- ☐ Record
- ☐ Edit
- ☐ Publish on Host
- ☐ Live on Directories
- ☐ Marketing
- ☐ Monetized

EPISODE *Planner*

TITLE

DISCRIPTION

GUEST **DATE**

SCRIPT/NOTES

KEYWORDS

CHECKLIST:
- ☐ Record
- ☐ Edit
- ☐ Publish on Host
- ☐ Live on Directories
- ☐ Marketing
- ☐ Monetized

EPISODE *Planner*

TITLE

DISCRIPTION

GUEST   DATE

SCRIPT/NOTES

KEYWORDS   CHECKLIST:
- ☐ Record   ☐ Live on Directories
- ☐ Edit   ☐ Marketing
- ☐ Publish on Host   ☐ Monetized

EPISODE *Planner*

TITLE

DISCRIPTION

GUEST   DATE

SCRIPT/NOTES

KEYWORDS   CHECKLIST:
- [ ] Record   - [ ] Live on Directories
- [ ] Edit   - [ ] Marketing
- [ ] Publish on Host - [ ] Monetized

EPISODE *Planner*

TITLE

DISCRIPTION

GUEST **DATE**

SCRIPT/NOTES

KEYWORDS

CHECKLIST:
- ☐ Record
- ☐ Edit
- ☐ Publish on Host
- ☐ Live on Directories
- ☐ Marketing
- ☐ Monetized

EPISODE *Planner*

TITLE

DISCRIPTION

GUEST   **DATE**

SCRIPT/NOTES

KEYWORDS

CHECKLIST:
- ☐ Record   ☐ Live on Directories
- ☐ Edit   ☐ Marketing
- ☐ Publish on Host ☐ Monetized

EPISODE *Planner*

TITLE

DISCRIPTION

GUEST **DATE**

SCRIPT/NOTES

KEYWORDS

CHECKLIST:
- ☐ Record
- ☐ Edit
- ☐ Publish on Host
- ☐ Live on Directories
- ☐ Marketing
- ☐ Monetized

EPISODE *Planner*

TITLE

DISCRIPTION

GUEST   DATE

SCRIPT/NOTES

KEYWORDS

CHECKLIST:
- ☐ Record   ☐ Live on Directories
- ☐ Edit   ☐ Marketing
- ☐ Publish on Host ☐ Monetized

EPISODE *Planner*

TITLE

DISCRIPTION

GUEST   DATE

SCRIPT/NOTES

KEYWORDS   CHECKLIST:
- [ ] Record   [ ] Live on Directories
- [ ] Edit   [ ] Marketing
- [ ] Publish on Host [ ] Monetized

EPISODE *Planner*

TITLE

DISCRIPTION

GUEST   DATE

SCRIPT/NOTES

KEYWORDS   CHECKLIST:
- ☐ Record   ☐ Live on Directories
- ☐ Edit   ☐ Marketing
- ☐ Publish on Host ☐ Monetized

EPISODE *Planner*

TITLE

DISCRIPTION

GUEST   **DATE**

SCRIPT/NOTES

KEYWORDS

CHECKLIST:
- ☐ Record   ☐ Live on Directories
- ☐ Edit   ☐ Marketing
- ☐ Publish on Host ☐ Monetized

EPISODE *Planner*

TITLE

DISCRIPTION

GUEST   DATE

SCRIPT/NOTES

KEYWORDS   CHECKLIST:
                        ☐ Record   ☐ Live on Directories
                        ☐ Edit   ☐ Marketing
                        ☐ Publish on Host ☐ Monetized

EPISODE *Planner*

TITLE

DISCRIPTION

GUEST   DATE

SCRIPT/NOTES

KEYWORDS   CHECKLIST:
- [ ] Record   [ ] Live on Directories
- [ ] Edit   [ ] Marketing
- [ ] Publish on Host [ ] Monetized

EPISODE *Planner*

TITLE

DISCRIPTION

GUEST   DATE

SCRIPT/NOTES

KEYWORDS   CHECKLIST:
                            ☐ Record   ☐ Live on Directories
                            ☐ Edit   ☐ Marketing
                            ☐ Publish on Host   ☐ Monetized

EPISODE *Planner*

TITLE

DISCRIPTION

GUEST   DATE

SCRIPT/NOTES

KEYWORDS   CHECKLIST:
- ☐ Record   ☐ Live on Directories
- ☐ Edit   ☐ Marketing
- ☐ Publish on Host ☐ Monetized

EPISODE *Planner*

TITLE

DISCRIPTION

GUEST   DATE

SCRIPT/NOTES

KEYWORDS   CHECKLIST:
- ☐ Record   ☐ Live on Directories
- ☐ Edit   ☐ Marketing
- ☐ Publish on Host ☐ Monetized

EPISODE *Planner*

TITLE

DISCRIPTION

GUEST   DATE

SCRIPT/NOTES

KEYWORDS   CHECKLIST:
- [ ] Record   - [ ] Live on Directories
- [ ] Edit   - [ ] Marketing
- [ ] Publish on Host - [ ] Monetized

EPISODE *Planner*

TITLE

DISCRIPTION

GUEST   DATE

SCRIPT/NOTES

KEYWORDS   CHECKLIST:
- ☐ Record   ☐ Live on Directories
- ☐ Edit   ☐ Marketing
- ☐ Publish on Host ☐ Monetized

EPISODE *Planner*

TITLE

DISCRIPTION

GUEST **DATE**

SCRIPT/NOTES

KEYWORDS

CHECKLIST:
- ☐ Record
- ☐ Edit
- ☐ Publish on Host
- ☐ Live on Directories
- ☐ Marketing
- ☐ Monetized

EPISODE *Planner*

TITLE

DISCRIPTION

GUEST   DATE

SCRIPT/NOTES

KEYWORDS   CHECKLIST:
- ☐ Record   ☐ Live on Directories
- ☐ Edit   ☐ Marketing
- ☐ Publish on Host ☐ Monetized

EPISODE *Planner*

TITLE

DISCRIPTION

GUEST   **DATE**

SCRIPT/NOTES

KEYWORDS

CHECKLIST:
- ☐ Record   ☐ Live on Directories
- ☐ Edit   ☐ Marketing
- ☐ Publish on Host ☐ Monetized

EPISODE *Planner*

TITLE

DISCRIPTION

GUEST   **DATE**

SCRIPT/NOTES

KEYWORDS   **CHECKLIST:**

☐ Record   ☐ Live on Directories
☐ Edit   ☐ Marketing
☐ Publish on Host   ☐ Monetized

EPISODE *Planner*

TITLE

DISCRIPTION

GUEST **DATE**

SCRIPT/NOTES

KEYWORDS

CHECKLIST:
- ☐ Record
- ☐ Edit
- ☐ Publish on Host
- ☐ Live on Directories
- ☐ Marketing
- ☐ Monetized

EPISODE *Planner*

TITLE

DISCRIPTION

GUEST **DATE**

SCRIPT/NOTES

KEYWORDS

CHECKLIST:
- ☐ Record
- ☐ Edit
- ☐ Publish on Host
- ☐ Live on Directories
- ☐ Marketing
- ☐ Monetized

EPISODE *Planner*

TITLE

DISCRIPTION

GUEST   DATE

SCRIPT/NOTES

KEYWORDS   CHECKLIST:
- [ ] Record   [ ] Live on Directories
- [ ] Edit   [ ] Marketing
- [ ] Publish on Host [ ] Monetized

EPISODE *Planner*

TITLE

DISCRIPTION

GUEST   DATE

SCRIPT/NOTES

KEYWORDS   CHECKLIST:
- [ ] Record   [ ] Live on Directories
- [ ] Edit   [ ] Marketing
- [ ] Publish on Host [ ] Monetized

EPISODE *Planner*

TITLE

DISCRIPTION

GUEST   DATE

SCRIPT/NOTES

KEYWORDS   CHECKLIST:
- ☐ Record   ☐ Live on Directories
- ☐ Edit   ☐ Marketing
- ☐ Publish on Host ☐ Monetized

EPISODE *Planner*

TITLE

DISCRIPTION

GUEST   DATE

SCRIPT/NOTES

KEYWORDS   CHECKLIST:
- ☐ Record   ☐ Live on Directories
- ☐ Edit   ☐ Marketing
- ☐ Publish on Host ☐ Monetized

EPISODE *Planner*

TITLE

DISCRIPTION

GUEST   DATE

SCRIPT/NOTES

KEYWORDS   CHECKLIST:
- ☐ Record   ☐ Live on Directories
- ☐ Edit   ☐ Marketing
- ☐ Publish on Host ☐ Monetized

EPISODE *Planner*

TITLE

DISCRIPTION

GUEST   DATE

SCRIPT/NOTES

KEYWORDS   CHECKLIST:
                 ☐ Record   ☐ Live on Directories
                 ☐ Edit   ☐ Marketing
                 ☐ Publish on Host   ☐ Monetized

EPISODE *Planner*

TITLE

DISCRIPTION

GUEST   DATE

SCRIPT/NOTES

KEYWORDS   CHECKLIST:
- [ ] Record   [ ] Live on Directories
- [ ] Edit   [ ] Marketing
- [ ] Publish on Host [ ] Monetized

EPISODE *Planner*

TITLE

DISCRIPTION

GUEST   **DATE**

SCRIPT/NOTES

KEYWORDS   **CHECKLIST:**

☐ Record   ☐ Live on Directories

☐ Edit   ☐ Marketing

☐ Publish on Host   ☐ Monetized

EPISODE *Planner*

TITLE

DISCRIPTION

GUEST   DATE

SCRIPT/NOTES

KEYWORDS   CHECKLIST:
- [ ] Record   [ ] Live on Directories
- [ ] Edit   [ ] Marketing
- [ ] Publish on Host [ ] Monetized

EPISODE *Planner*

TITLE

DISCRIPTION

GUEST   **DATE**

SCRIPT/NOTES

KEYWORDS

CHECKLIST:
- ☐ Record   ☐ Live on Directories
- ☐ Edit   ☐ Marketing
- ☐ Publish on Host ☐ Monetized

EPISODE *Planner*

TITLE

DISCRIPTION

GUEST **DATE**

SCRIPT/NOTES

KEYWORDS

CHECKLIST:
- ☐ Record   ☐ Live on Directories
- ☐ Edit   ☐ Marketing
- ☐ Publish on Host   ☐ Monetized

Notes:

Notes:

Notes:

Notes:

Notes:

Notes:

Notes:

ALSO BY JERRY

This book is dedicated entirely to teaching you all I know about starting a podcast. It is organized in 7 simple steps that walk you from selecting a niche to finally hitting publish. Read on for straight to the point guidance along with plenty of tips and tricks.

www.ingramcontent.com/pod-product-compliance
Lightning Source LLC
LaVergne TN
LVHW052234110526
838202LV00095B/221